CHRISTMAS

Dana Phillips

DECEMBER

Full Color Calendar Header

3
Full Color
Posters

December can be an exhilarating (and exhausting) time in the classroom — a time when Santa Claus is on many little minds and everything seems to unfold in a profusion of red and green. It's a time of winter wonderlands, of sugarplums and candy canes, of prancing reindeer and boughs of holly.

Unlike any other month, December is a challenge and a chance to carry students through it all with a holiday spirit and a sleigh full of learning!

**120 Full Color
Reward Seals**

**20 Pages of Student
Duplicating Masters**

**32 Page Teacher
Resource Guide**

6 Foot Black and White Banner for Your Kids to Color!

ACTIVITY CALENDAR BOARD

...A jolly activity for every day!

DECEMBER

Write a Christmas poem.	2	3	4	5	6
7	8	9	10	11	12
13	14	15	16	17	18
19	20	21	22	23	24
25	26	27	28	29	30
31					

To make:
1. Place the **December** header (in middle of book) at the top of a bulletin board.
2. Cut 8 pieces of construction paper in fourths.
3. Fold 31 pieces in half. Number 1-31 on the front of the flap.
4. Copy and cut out the 31 activities on the next page.
5. Glue them inside the 31 folded papers. (Students can lightly color first.)
6. Arrange them in order on board for an "Activity-a-Day!"

Draw a picture of your family on Christmas morning.	Design a special Christmas tree ornament.	Draw a map for Santa to use on Christmas Eve.	List as many words as you can that begin with HO!	Finish this sentence: Santa asked Rudolph to help because...
Draw a picture that tells about your favorite Christmas song.	Draw a mantel with a stocking for each person in your family.	List 10 things Santa does the day before Christmas.	Write 10 Christmas words. Under-line each vowel. Circle each consonant.	List 10 words that can describe a Christmas tree.
Write a menu for Christmas dinner.	Pretend you are an elf. How would you help Santa?	Write a Christmas poem.	Write a story about spending Christmas in another country.	Draw a partridge in a pear tree.
Draw a picture of the gift you most want!	List 5 ways you can share more this Christmas.	Finish this story: Once upon a time at the North Pole...	Draw a big present tied with Christmas ribbon. Label it.	Draw a picture of your Christmas Eve dream.
Describe the snack you will leave for Santa.	List 5 places Santa might shop for gifts.	Draw a green Christmas tree. Decorate it just for you.	Write 5 words from the letters in December.	Write the names of Santa's reindeer.
Design a Christmas card for Santa.	Design a Hanukkah card.	Write a list of your favorite holiday songs.	Write a sentence that begins with each letter in December.	List 5 facts about Santa. / Write a letter to Santa.

Duplicate this page. Cut out each activity.

DECEMBER CALENDARS

Classroom Calendar

...To record the 12 days of Christmas and more!

1. Use the **December** header (in the middle of the book). Place at the top of a bulletin board.
2. On a colorful piece of posterboard, use a thick black marker to draw vertical and horizontal lines to make squares for each day of the month.
3. Across the top write the days of the week:

SUNDAY	MONDAY	TUESDAY	WEDNESDAY	THURSDAY	FRIDAY	SATURDAY

4. Use the patterns to cut trees and/or stockings from colored paper.

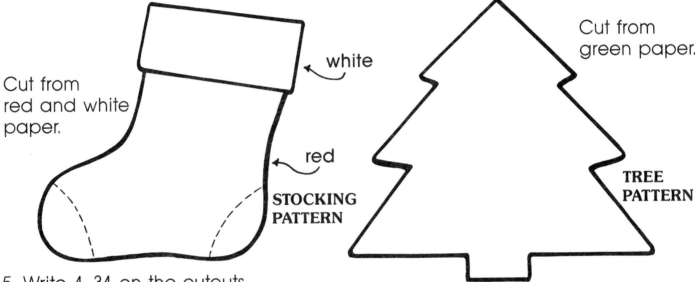

white

Cut from red and white paper.

red

STOCKING PATTERN

Cut from green paper.

TREE PATTERN

5. Write 1-31 on the cutouts.
6. Let students take turns placing the numbers on the calendar each day.

Individual Student Calendars

1. Duplicate an individual student calendar on colored tagboard for each student.
2. Duplicate a page of calendar stickers for each student.
3. Students can color calendar and stickers.
4. Have students write 1-31 on their calendars.

Duplicating Page #33

Duplicating Page #34

Or use: IFChart Seals 4311

"TREE" MENDOUS TREATS FOR KIDS

Awards December is a month for sharing. Share these "treats" to reward good work, good behavior and good attitude — for GOODNESS SAKE!

1. Duplicate a stack of award sheets (duplicating page 35) on colored paper.
2. Cut in half and give to students to reward good work or good behavior all through the month.

Or use:

Duplicating Page #35

Christmas Wear 'Em Award Badges IF4411

Christmas Reward Seals IF4204

BUILD SELF-ESTEEM!

 **Individual Incentive Chart**

1. Duplicate a copy of page 36 on colored tagboard for each student.
2. Set individual and class goals.
3. Award stickers as goals are met.
4. When chart is filled, send home!

Duplicating Page #36

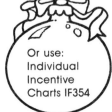 Or use: Individual Incentive Charts IF354

The Parent Connection

1. Duplicate a copy of December's **Help-at-Home Activity Calendar** on colored paper for each student.
2. Send home to parents at the first of the month.

Duplicating Page #37

DEAR

BULLETIN BOARD

1. Cover a large board with blue paper (sky). Attach a band of white paper across lower third of board to make snow. (Tear top edge for uneven look of snow.)

2. Cut red letters: **DEAR SANTA CLAUS**

3. Place letters at top of board.

4. Use an opaque projector to enlarge Santa, child and mailbox. Color Santa's suit and hat red and white and his boots black. Color child's hair, coat, pants, boots and mittens appropriate colors. Color mailbox blue.

5. Place Santa on left end of board. Place child and mailbox at right side.

6. On two white envelopes write: **To: Santa Claus North Pole**

   Place a stamp on each or draw one.
   Place one envelope in Santa's hand — and one in child's hand.

7. Duplicate a copy of page 38 for each student.

8. Have each student write a letter to Santa. Then, trim edges and color the border.

9. Attach each page to the board. (You could mount them on green paper.)

10. When board is taken down, send papers home — or — stack papers, punch holes, add construction paper cover and tie with yarn to make class collection.

Duplicating Page #38

SANTA CLAUS

Santa's List
Word Search

1. Duplicate a copy of page 39 for each student.
2. Have students cut on dotted line to separate activities.

Duplicating Page #39

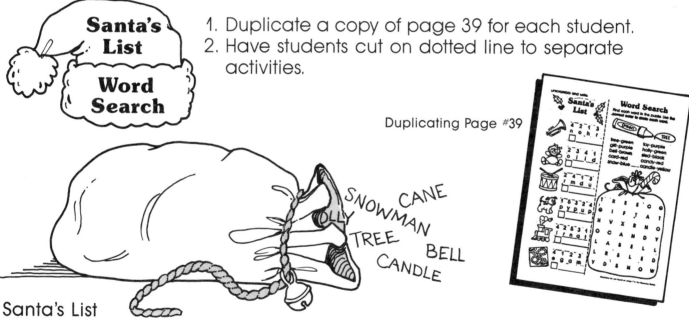

Santa's List
1. Have students unscramble the words by using the numbers and write the words on the lines.
2. Older students can alphabetize list by writing 1-6 in the box by each word.
3. Students can use each word in a sentence or all words in a paragraph on separate paper.

Word Search
1. Have students find each word in the puzzle and use the correct color to circle each word.
2. Have students select five words to illustrate on a separate paper and use each of the words in a sentence.

HERE COMES SANTA CLAUS
A Christmas Gameboard

Help Santa find your house!

Look out! A snowstorm! Lose a turn!

Rudolph's red nose shines brightly! Move ahead 2 spaces!

Oops! A toy fell from Santa's bag! Go back 1 space.

A CHRISTMAS GAMEBOARD

... A vocabulary skills game!

To make:

1. Copy the gameboard (page 8). Color with markers and paste on larger red posterboard.
2. Or use an opaque projector to enlarge, color and paste to make a much larger board for more than 2 players.

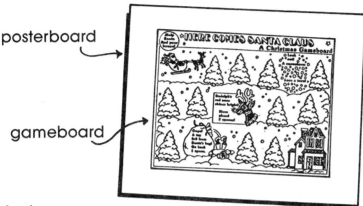

posterboard

gameboard

GAMEBOARD CAN BE USED FOR ANY SKILL!

Cut and wrap around spool.

MARKER   PATTERN

Markers:

1. Use the pattern to cut several Santas from white construction paper.
2. Color Santa red and white.
3. Wrap each Santa around an empty spool and glue.
4. Place Santa markers in center by gameboard.

HERE COMES SANTA CLAUS!

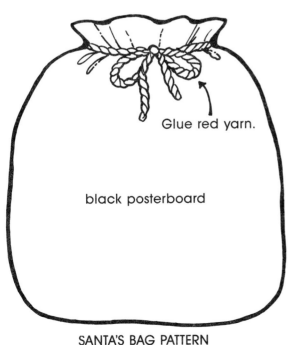

Glue red yarn.

black posterboard

SANTA'S BAG PATTERN

To play:

1. Enlarge bag pattern and cut from black posterboard. Glue red yarn for tie.
2. Copy page 10. Color the pictures. Paste on a piece of posterboard. Cut pictures and words apart on puzzle lines.
3. Place picture sections on bag so each can be seen.
4. Place word sections in stack by bag.
5. Let two or more students take turns:
   a. Pick up word card and read aloud.
   b. Place by correct picture on bag.
   c. If correct, move number of spaces on card.
   d. If incorrect, lose turn.
   e. Players rotate until winner reaches home.

Playing Cards for Christmas Gameboard

Copy and color pictures. Paste on posterboard.
Cut pictures and words apart on puzzle lines.

elf
1 space

stocking
1 space

snowman
2 spaces

holly
2 spaces

gift
2 spaces

ornament
1 space

reindeer
1 space

sleigh
1 space

tree
1 space

chimney
2 spaces

wreath
1 space

candy
1 space

candle
1 space

Santa
1 space

December Holiday Kit IF8604

SANTA CLAUS

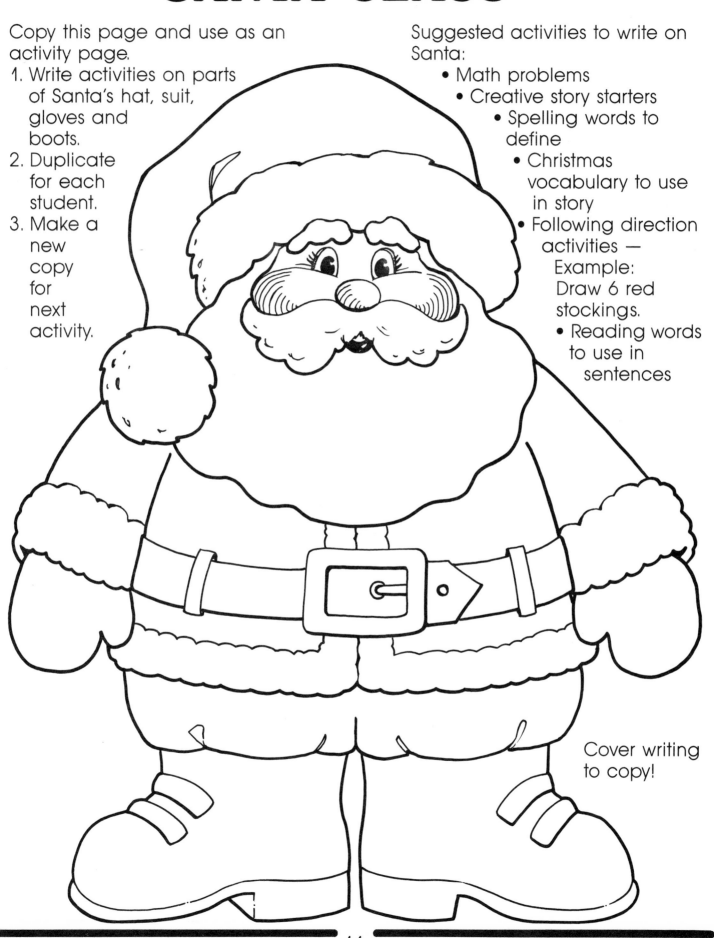

Copy this page and use as an activity page.

1. Write activities on parts of Santa's hat, suit, gloves and boots.
2. Duplicate for each student.
3. Make a new copy for next activity.

Suggested activities to write on Santa:
- Math problems
- Creative story starters
- Spelling words to define
- Christmas vocabulary to use in story
- Following direction activities — Example: Draw 6 red stockings.
- Reading words to use in sentences

Cover writing to copy!

RUDOLPH, WITH YOUR NOSE SO BRIGHT...

Bulletin Board
Feature student work with this board!

Use red glitter.

RUDOLPH PATTERN

Bright and Shiny Work!

1. Cover a board with green paper.
2. Attach red letters at top: **BRIGHT AND SHINY WORK!**
3. Enlarge Rudolph pattern on brown paper using an opaque projector.
   Use red glitter to cover nose!
4. Cut several circles from red construction paper. Cover with red glitter.
5. Attach Rudolph on left side of board. Use circles (noses) to feature student work!

Reindeer Names

A Center Activity

1. Use the antler pattern to cut 10 brown antlers.
2. On one antler write: Dasher, Dancer, Prancer, Vixen, Comet, Cupid, Donner, Blitzen and Rudolph.
3. Write a scrambled reindeer name on each of the other antlers. Example: e m o t c (Comet)
4. Place the 10 antlers in a red pocket folder.
5. Write **Unscramble Santa's Reindeer!** on cover and place in center.

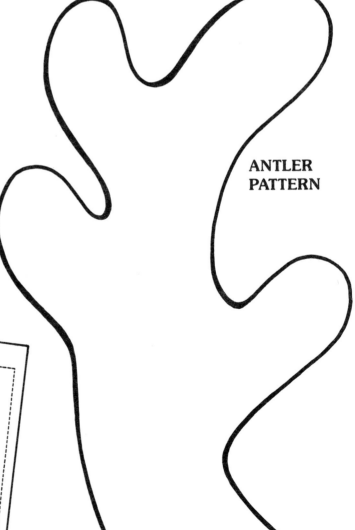

ANTLER PATTERN

Reindeer Hat

1. Duplicate a copy of page 40 on brown paper for each student.
2. Have students cut antlers and strips. Staple strips to make a head-band; then staple antlers to it.

Duplicating Page #40

WON'T YOU GUIDE MY SLEIGH TONIGHT?

Let Rudolph and friends add to the Christmas learning fun!

Reindeer Mobile

1. Use an opaque projector to enlarge reindeer and antlers on brown posterboard. Use yellow or gold for antlers.
2. Use a black marker to outline.
3. Cut a red circle and paste for a "Rudolph" nose.
4. Use bell pattern to cut 6 bells from colorful paper.
5. Write an activity on each:
   - Write a letter to Rudolph.
   - Draw a picture of your favorite reindeer.
   - Make up new names for Santa's reindeer.
   - Help the reindeer find your house! Draw a map from the North Pole to your house.
   - Pretend you are one of Santa's reindeer. Write a story about Christmas Eve.
   - Write a reindeer poem.
6. Punch holes in antlers and bells. Tie with red yarn to make a mobile. Hang over center or display on board.

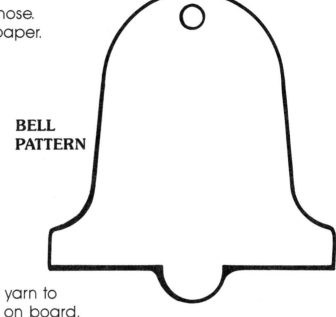

BELL PATTERN

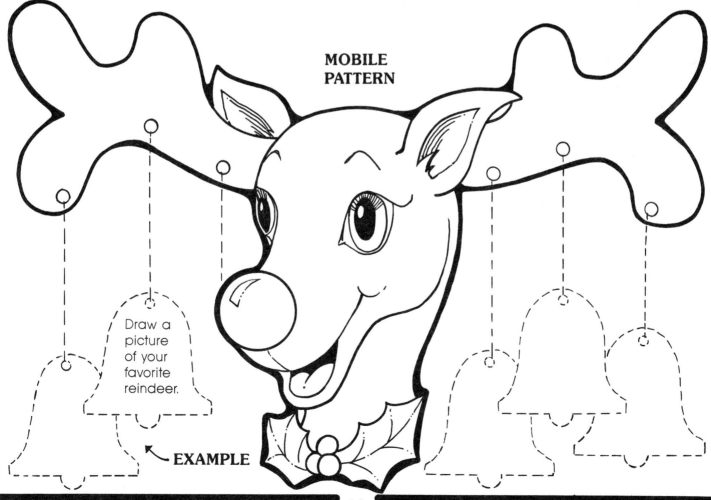

MOBILE PATTERN

Draw a picture of your favorite reindeer.

← **EXAMPLE**

SANTA'S WORKSHOP

...Where Santa's elves are busy planning more learning fun!

Creative Story Starters

Place hats in center.

SANTA'S HAT PATTERN

white

red

white

1. Use the pattern to cut and paste six hats from red and white paper.
2. Use a black marker to write a story starter on each red hat and the vocabulary words on the white trim.
   - It was Christmas Eve and the elves were busy…**(packing, hurry, suit, boots, North Pole, excited)**
   - Santa Claus put on his new red and white suit and…**(jolly, Ho! Ho! Ho!, Mrs. Claus, list, sleigh, presents)**
   - The tree glowed with hundreds of lights…**(green, star, angel, ornaments, shiny, huge)**
   - The reindeer ran out from their barn to…**(eight, Rudolph, lively, fly, hooves, antlers)**
   - All the boys and girls were excited because tonight…**(bedtime, sleepy, dreams, toys, steps, chimney)**
   - The woods were beautiful in the Christmas moonlight…**(snow, glisten, Frosty, snowman, trees, sleighbells)**

Mitten Math

1. Cut a stack of mittens from black construction paper. Use half as right mitten — turn other half over for left mitten.
2. Write math problems on left mitten with a white crayon.
3. Write answers on right mitten.
4. Place in center.

7 x 8   56

MATH DRILL!

MITTEN PATTERN

Santa's Workshop

1. Duplicate a copy of page 41 for each student.
2. Have students find and color each "hidden" picture in Santa's workshop.

Duplicating Page #41

Santa Puppet

1. Duplicate a copy of page 42 for each student.
2. Color and cut Santa puppet pieces.
3. Paste on brown paper lunch bag.

Duplicating Page #42

 14

BANNER

An Art Center Idea!

Santa Welcome Here!

ART

Hall Display

1. Have students color the banner in the back of the book. Attach to the hall wall.

2. Place in art center:
   • A stack of red construction paper stockings
   • White construction paper stocking tops
   • An assortment of small fabric pieces

3. Have students paste white top on red stocking and paste fabric pieces on stocking like a patchwork quilt.

4. Write each student's name in glue on white tops and sprinkle with glitter.

5. Display student patchwork stockings in hall under the banner.

PATCHWORK STOCKING

GLITTER

FABRIC

STOCKING PATTERN

STOCKING STUFFERS

Idea!

Here is an idea for helping students reach important goals — and still feel the holiday excitement!

Motivational Activity

Duplicating
Page #43

1. Duplicate a copy of page 43 for each student.
2. Have students color and cut the stocking and four "stuffers", cut a slit on top of stocking and write their names.
3. Set four important class goals.
4. Designate a stuffer as a reward for each goal.
   Example: Complete Science Booklet = Teddy Bear
             Good Behavior = Candy Cane
5. As students meet goals, have them place stuffer in slit. Glue front of tab.
6. When all four stuffers are earned — stocking goes home!

Story Starters

A Center Idea!

Story Starters

1. Use the stocking pattern on page 15 to make a large red posterboard stocking, or use a fabric stocking.
2. Use the candy cane pattern on page 17 to cut 6 candy canes from white posterboard.
3. Use a thick red marker to outline canes and to write a starter on each:
   - There were only two more shopping days until Christmas, so…
   - Santa's elves quickly gathered the gifts and…
   - The twins had never seen snow before, so they…
   - The kids thought the gingerbread cookie moved on the pan…
   - Late Christmas Eve, the children heard steps on the roof…
   - Everyone was so surprised at whom they saw standing by the fireplace…
4. Place candy canes in stocking in center.

Stocking Sort

A Posterboard Activity!

green posterboard

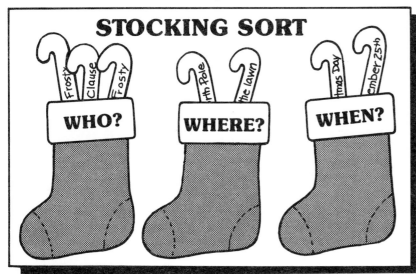

STOCKING SORT

WHO? WHERE? WHEN?

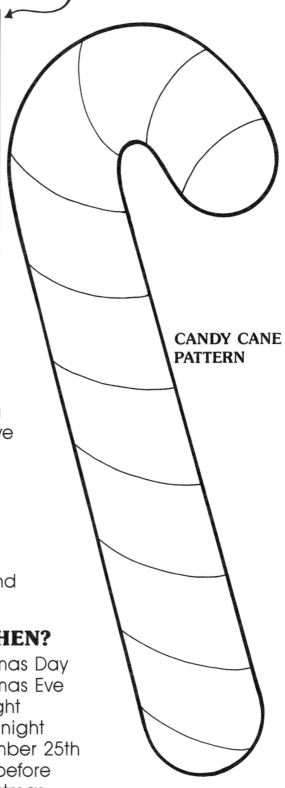

CANDY CANE PATTERN

To make:

1. Use a full piece of green posterboard.
2. Attach red letters - **STOCKING SORT** - at the top of posterboard.
3. Use stocking pattern on page 15 to cut three red stockings with white tops.
4. Put glue around the edges and paste in a row on posterboard to make pockets. Leave top open.
5. Write: **WHO? - WHERE? - WHEN?** on white stocking tops.
6. Make a large candy cane like the one shown and cut 18 canes from white construction paper.
7. Use a thick red marker to outline canes and write on each:

WHO?	**WHERE?**	**WHEN?**
Santa Claus	North Pole	Christmas Day
elves	in the chimney	Christmas Eve
Rudolph	on the lawn	midnight
children	up on the	foggy night
Mrs. Claus	housetop	December 25th
Frosty	in Santa's sleigh	night before
	under the tree	Christmas

8. Write **WHO? - WHERE?** or **WHEN?** on back of canes for self checking.
9. Place all in center.
10. Have students place canes in correct stockings.

O'CHRISTMAS TREE...

Math Tree

1. Draw a large tree like the one shown on green posterboard.
2. Stick large star stickers around border of tree.
3. Cut a stack of red construction paper cards. Write subtraction fact problems on each.
4. Provide several small items as markers.
5. Place in center. Have students: choose a card and move marker from START the same number of stars as the answer. The first player to STOP wins.
6. Use gameboard for any skill. Add dice to roll for number of spaces.

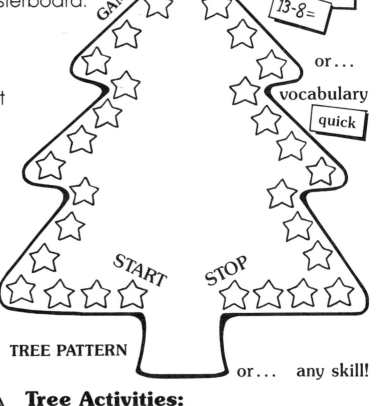

GAMEBOARD   subtraction cards

$5-2=$

$13-8=$

or...

vocabulary

quick

START   STOP

TREE PATTERN   or...   any skill!

Tree Activities:

Write as many words as you can from the letters in:

C H R I S T M A S   T R E E.

Write a Christmas tree poem.
Write a list of words that contain **ee**.
Write six steps in decorating a Christmas tree.
Draw a forest with $15-4$ green trees.
Write a story about how a small seed becomes a Christmas tree.

Christmas Tree Lane

A center activity!

1. Find a large shirt box about 2 or 3 inches deep.
2. Cover the top and sides with white cotton.
3. Use tree pattern above to cut 6 green trees plus one larger one.
4. Write an activity on each tree.
5. Write **CHRISTMAS TREE LANE** on the large tree.
6. Fasten a popsickle stick to the back of each tree trunk.
7. Cut 7 slots through the cotton and box top.
8. Stick each tree (stick) into a slot.
9. Place in center!

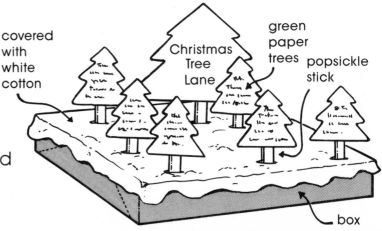

covered with white cotton

Christmas Tree Lane

green paper trees   popsickle stick

box

O'CHRISTMAS TREE!

Phonics Trees

An activity board that's easy to change!

1. Cover a small board with blue or black paper.
2. Tear white paper and place along bottom for snow, or use cotton.
3. Cut several large green triangles from construction paper.
4. Cut as many brown rectangles for tree trunks.
5. Paste together and attach trees to board along top of snow.
6. Attach red letters — **SOUNDS OF CHRISTMAS** - at top of board.
7. Cut and attach yellow moon.
8. Add star stickers.
9. Write a phonics sound that the class is studying on each tree trunk.
10. Have students bring pictures representing sounds and paste on trees.
11. Change trees during month.

gold star stickers

SOUNDS OF CHRISTMAS

br   ee   le   oi

ABC Tree

Paste rows of sparkly tree garland.

1 2 3 4 5 6 7 8

A center activity!

1. Make a large tree like the one on page 18 from large green posterboard.
2. Use a marker to draw 8 circles forming a path down the tree. Number 1-8.
3. Paste several garlands of sparkly tree decorations across the tree.
4. Cut 8 colorful circles from construction paper.
5. Write a word on each:
   Christmas   tree   angel
   ornaments   lights   star
   green   presents
6. Place "Christmas balls" and tree in center.
7. Have students place words on number circles to put words in ABC order.

TRIM THE TREE!

3-D Tree

An Art Center Idea!

To make:
Place a large piece of green construction paper for each student in the art center. Have each student:

1. Fold paper in half, fold in half again — and fold in half again!

2. Draw a half-tree pattern on the folded paper.

cut

2.

3. Unfold tree and lay in a double thickness.
4. Glue the two ends together.

5.

5. Now open to make a circle.

6. Glue each tree section to the tree section next to it.

6.

1.

folded double

3.

glue

4.

glitter

7.

7. Dab tree with glue and cover with glitter.

ORNAMENTS

Silver Fans

To make:
1. Give each student a 5" x 7" piece of heavy-duty aluminum foil and a piece of red or green yarn.
2. Have students:
   a. Fold foil like an accordian.

   b. Hold folds together and punch hole in center.

   c. Put yarn through hole and tie knot.
   d. Open ends to show fan.
   e. Tie on tree with a bow made of yarn.

Curly Cutes

To make:
1. Give each student a green or red circle (about 5 inches in diameter) made of construction paper and a piece of red or green yarn.
2. Have students:
   a. Start at the outside of circle and cut the paper in a spiral.
   b. Punch a hole in the inside circle.
   c. Tie yarn and hang on tree.

Punch hole.

Tie with yarn.

A Door Decoration

BRIGHT LIGHTS OF CHRISTMAS

1. Make a large tree like the one on page 18 and cut from green paper. Attach to classroom door.
2. Attach red letters - **BRIGHT LIGHTS OF CHRISTMAS** - at top of door.
3. Use light pattern to cut a light for each student using a variety of bright colors.
4. Use a black marker to add details.
5. Have students write their names on lights with markers.
6. Attach red yarn in rows across tree.
7. Attach "lights" on yarn to make colorful strings of lights.

String of Lights **A center activity for many skills!**

1. Attach colorful yarn along chalk tray or low on a wall like a clothesline.
2. Use light pattern to cut a stack of colorful lights. Write an activity on each.
3. Attach tree ornament hooks to tops of lights.
4. Students can unhook a light to choose an activity.

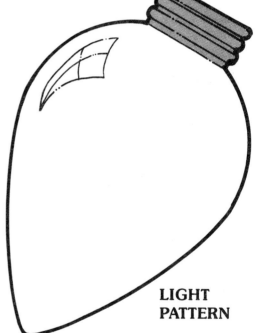

LIGHT PATTERN

Activities

- If you had a string of 16 lights and 4 burned out, how many lights would be burning? Draw a string with that number of lights.
- Write as many words as possible that rhyme with light.
- Draw a colorful light for every year of your age. Write your age in each light.
- List 8 things that light helps you do.
- Draw a Christmas tree with $8 + 7$ lights on it.
- Write a sentence using each word: bright, light, string, bulb.
- Name 10 things that give off light.
- Write a story about what Santa did when Rudolph's nose burned out.

'TWAS THE NIGHT BEFORE CHRISTMAS...

Handwriting ➤ **Not Even a Mouse**

1. Use the mouse pattern to cut a stack of colorful mice from construction paper.
2. Use a black marker for outline and details.
3. Copy each passage from **THE NIGHT BEFORE CHRISTMAS** on a mouse.
4. Place mice in center.
5. Have students copy passages for handwriting practice.

MOUSE PATTERN

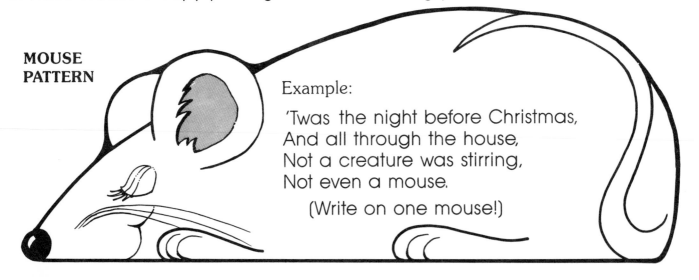

Example:

'Twas the night before Christmas,
And all through the house,
Not a creature was stirring,
Not even a mouse.

(Write on one mouse!)

 **Oral Activity**

A class poem project*

1. Early in the month assign 2 or 3 lines from "The Night Before Christmas" to each student in the class.
2. Ask students to practice their lines for a week.
3. Start daily class recitation of poem; each day improving!
4. By mid-month, class can easily say poem — each student saying his/her lines at correct time.
5. A fun daily activity! Great for visitors and parents!

 **Activity Sheet**

A Long Winter's Nap

Duplicating Page #44

1. Duplicate a copy of page 44 for each student and place in pocket folder.
2. Write: **A LONG WINTER'S NAP** on the cover and place in center.
3. Have students draw a picture and write a story about a Christmas Eve dream.

***Reward with mouse treats: cheese cubes and mini-crackers!**

VISIONS OF SUGARPLUMS!

...A delicious way to learn synonyms!

Peppermint Pick

To make:
1. Cover a large cardboard pizza wheel with a round piece of white posterboard.
2. Use a red marker to:
   - Make a red center in the "candy".
   - Make 8 red swirls to divide the "candy" into 8 sections.
   - Write a word from Row I in each section.
   - Write the words from Row II on 8 wooden clothespins.

Row I: present, chilly, share, happy, children, small, silent, housetop

Row II: gift, cold, give, jolly, kids, tiny, quiet, roof

3. Place all in center.
4. Have students clip clothespins to match synonyms.

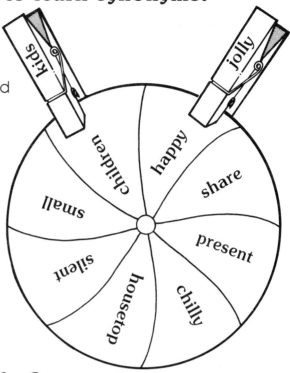

An Art Center Idea!

Sugarplum House

Need:
- cotton
- glue and glitter
- small milk cartons
- colorful construction paper

To make:

Have students:
a. Cover "roof" with glue and cotton.
b. Cover sides with glue and paper.
c. Use glue and glitter to decorate house.
d. Use glue and paper to add doors, windows and more!

Display on cotton-covered table!

Candy Cane Compounds

A Center Activity!

To make:
1. Use the candy cane pattern on page 17 to cut 10 canes from white tagboard.
2. Outline canes with a red marker. Add a line in the middle.
3. Use a red marker to write a compound word (one part on each side of line):

house/top	gum/drop
snow/man	pepper/mint
ever/green	rein/deer
fire/place	ginger/bread
mistle/toe	sugar/plum

4. Cut each cane in half on the line.
5. Place a candy tin or box in center.
6. Have students match compound words.

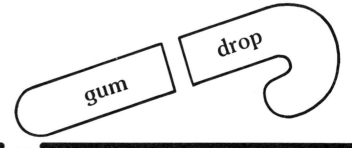

Run, Run, As Fast As You Can!

A Posterboard Activity for Story Sequence!

HOUSE
PATTERN

FOX
PATTERN

Run, Run, as Fast as You Can!

To make:

1. Use a full piece of colorful posterboard.
2. Write across top - RUN, RUN, AS FAST AS YOU CAN!
3. Using an opaque projector, enlarge the house and the fox patterns shown above. Color with bright markers.
4. Use gingerbread pattern on page 25 to cut 8 of them from brown construction paper.
5. Use a black marker to add eyes, nose and mouth and write a sentence on each:
   - One day a little woman decided to make a gingerbread man.
   - She used raisins for his eyes, nose and mouth.
   - Next, she used gumdrops for his buttons.
   - She put the gingerbread man in the oven to bake.
   - When she opened the oven the gingerbread man jumped out and ran away!
   - The gingerbread man met a cow and a cat as he ran through the field.
   - But then he asked a fox to take him across the river.
   - The fox tricked the gingerbread man and gobbled him up.
6. On the board, number 1-8 in a trail from the house to the fox.
7. Place all in center. Have students lay gingerbread men on numbers to put story in correct order.

You Can't Catch Me!

Christmas Party Invitation

To make:

1. Cut a gingerbread man from brown construction paper for each student using the pattern.
2. Have students:

   Write: **PLEASE COME!**
   CHRISTMAS PARTY
   DATE _____
   TIME _____

- Outline gingerbread man and eyes, nose and mouth with glue.
- Sprinkle with red glitter.
- Take home to parents!

red glitter

Stuffed Gingerbread Man

An Art Center Idea!

Students will love to make and take this home!

To make:

1. Have students bring a large brown grocery bag.
2. Provide large gingerbread pattern, hole puncher, red yarn, newspaper and red paper.
3. Students:
   a. Trace pattern on bag.
   b. Cut **double**!
   c. Punch holes around border.
   d. Stitch with red yarn.
   e. Leave opening to stuff with crumpled torn newspaper.
   f. Stitch closed.
   g. Cut and paste red circles for eyes, nose and mouth.

red yarn

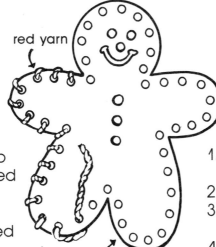
brown paper bag

GINGERBREAD MAN PATTERN

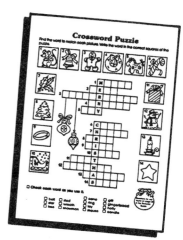

PLEASE COME!

CHRISTMAS PARTY!

DATE _____

TIME _____

Crossword Puzzle

Duplicating Page #45

1. Duplicate a copy of page 45 for each student.
2. Place in pocket folder.
3. Cut and paste a brown gingerbread man for cover.
4. Write **GINGERBREAD PUZZLE** on cover.
5. Place in center.

BERRY PATTERN

An Art Center Idea!

Picture Wreath

Paper Plate

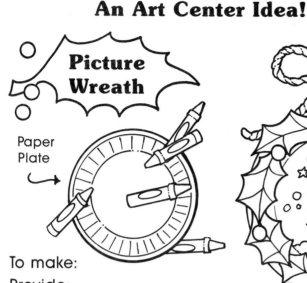

HOLLY PATTERN

To make:

Provide:

1. A paper plate for each student
2. Holly and berry patterns
3. Green and red construction paper
4. Yarn

Have students:

1. Draw a colorful Christmas scene on the inner circle of the paper plate.
2. Cut and paste holly and berries around rim of plate to form a wreath frame.
3. Punch hole at top and tie yarn to display.

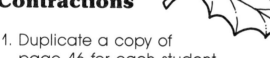

Contractions

1. Duplicate a copy of page 46 for each student.
2. Place in a pocket folder.
3. Write **CHRISTMAS CONTRACTIONS** on cover.
4. Place in center.

Duplicating Page #46

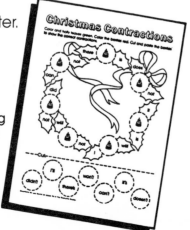

Pop-Up Christmas Card

Provide for each student:

1. A copy of duplicating page #47
2. A piece of green or red construction paper — folded horizontally in half

Have students:

1. Color and cut pop-up card.
2. Paste tabs on inside crease of construction paper.
3. Fold card closed and decorate card cover.
4. On inside of card, write holiday message and sign.

Duplicating Page #47

Sharing and Caring

Creative Writing!

Posters

1. Display the three posters in the holiday center.
2. Enlarge the bows on colorful paper.
3. Write the directions on each bow and attach to a poster.

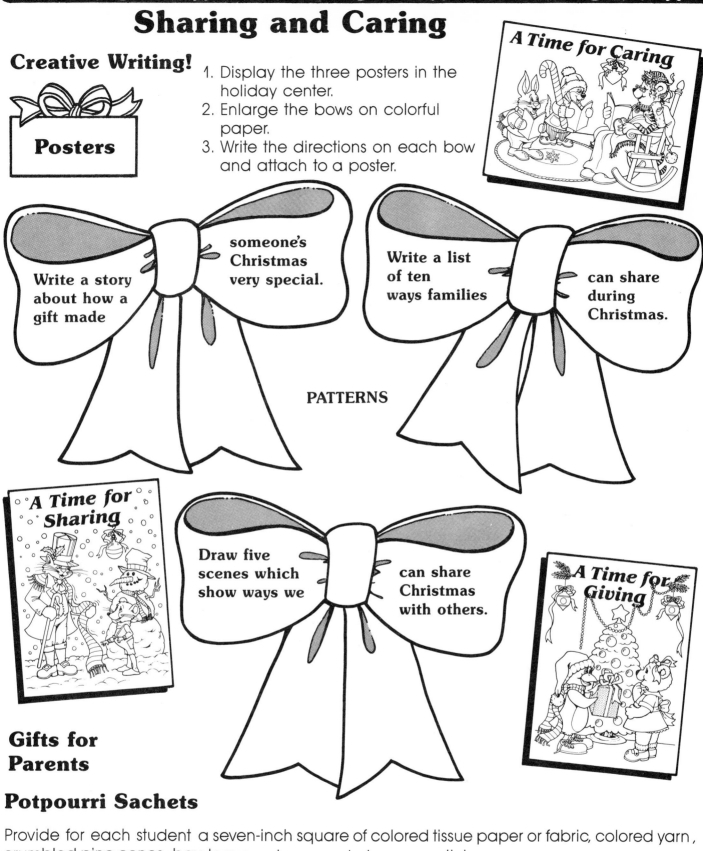

A Time for Caring

Write a story about how a gift made someone's Christmas very special.

Write a list of ten ways families can share during Christmas.

PATTERNS

A Time for Sharing

Draw five scenes which show ways we can share Christmas with others.

A Time for Giving

Gifts for Parents

Potpourri Sachets

Provide for each student a seven-inch square of colored tissue paper or fabric, colored yarn, crumbled pine cones, bay leaves, cloves and cinnamon sticks.

Have students:

1. Place crumbled mixture in center of tissue or fabric.
2. Gather the corners and tie with yarn.
3. Take home as a gift.

The 12 Days of Christmas A Center Activity Board!

To make:

1. Use a full piece of red or green posterboard (vertical).
2. Use a marker to write on top:
   THE TWELVE DAYS OF CHRISTMAS
3. Copy, color and cut out the 12 pictures on page 29.
4. Paste pictures in 1-12 order down left side of board.
5. Cut 12 tagboard strips. Write one line on each:
   On the first day: A partridge in a pear tree
   On the second day: Two turtle doves
   On the third day: Three French hens
   On the fourth day: Four colly birds
   On the fifth day: Five golden rings
   On the sixth day: Six geese a-laying
   On the seventh day: Seven swans a-swimming
   On the eighth day: Eight maids a-milking
   On the ninth day: Nine ladies dancing

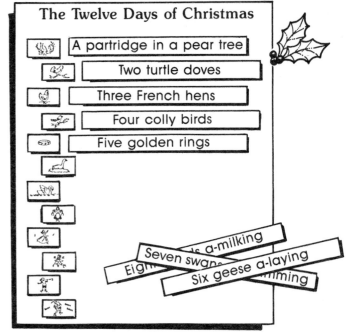

The Twelve Days of Christmas

- A partridge in a pear tree
- Two turtle doves
- Three French hens
- Four colly birds
- Five golden rings

Seven swans a-milking
Eight... a-milking
Six geese a-laying
...mming

On the tenth day: Ten lords a-leaping
On the eleventh day: Eleven pipers piping
On the twelfth day: Twelve drummers drumming

6. Place all in center.
7. Have students place strips in 1-12 order by correct pictures.

Music Book

To make:

1. Duplicate copies of pages 48 and 49 on white paper — and page 50 on white tagboard or construction paper.
2. Have students:
   a. Color all pictures on pages 48 and 49 and the border on page 50.
   b. Cut pictures apart, place in order.
   c. Cut cover strip from bottom of page 50.
   d. Fold and place pictures inside, staple as booklet.
   e. Cut out booklet frame on page 50.
   f. Staple booklet in center of frame.

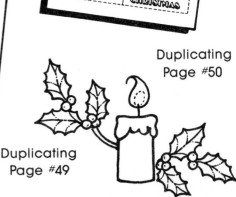

Duplicating Page #50

Duplicating Page #49

Duplicating Page #48

Color and cut.

A MUSICAL CHRISTMAS PLAY

...For the entire class

Players: Narrator **Santa Claus**
children **reindeer (Wear reindeer hats - page 40.)**
parents **chorus**

Read narration or have a student read it.
Have students create dialogue at designated points.
Have chorus sing songs at designated points.
Each performance will be different as students individualize dialogue!

Narrator: 'Twas the night before Christmas! The Taylor family was looking out their window watching a sleigh full of carolers go by. They could hear the bells across their snowy lawn. **(Sing - Jingle Bells.)** The Taylor children were just putting the last ornaments on their tree. They stood back to look and said: **(Dialogue) (Sing - O Christmas Tree.)** Soon Mr. & Mrs. Taylor said it was bedtime. **(Dialogue)** As they went to bed the children skipped and laughed and sang. **(Sing - Santa Claus is Coming to Town.)** Finally, they settled into bed and turned off the lights. Lying in bed they talked excitedly about what they hoped Santa would bring them. **(Dialogue)** But suddenly they heard a loud bump on their roof. They ran to the window and looked up. They couldn't believe their eyes! **(Dialogue) (Sing - Up on the Housetop.)** Santa told his reindeer to stand still and wait for him. **(Dialogue)** He slid down the chimney and quickly went to work filling stockings and leaving gifts under the tree. As he worked he said, "Ho! Ho! Ho!" again and again. Then just as quickly as he came, Santa went up the chimney and jumped into his sleigh. As the reindeer flew away Santa exclaimed, "Merry Christmas and goodnight."
The Taylor children ran back to bed and fell quickly to sleep. In just a wink, it seemed, it was Christmas morning. As the Taylor family walked down the stairs, Mr. and Mrs. Taylor asked if the children had heard or seen anything unusual during the night. The children said they hadn't! **(Dialogue)** Now do you think the children were just pretending...or was it really just a dream? **(Sing - We Wish You a Merry Christmas.)**

An eight day festival...   **Begins about the middle of December**

A Board Idea!

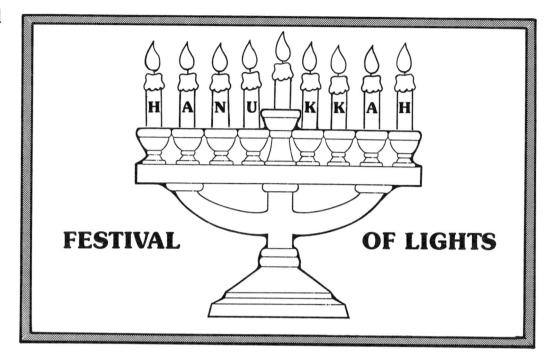

FESTIVAL   **OF LIGHTS**

To make:

1. Cover board with blue paper.
2. Using an opaque projector, enlarge Menorah pattern on page 51. Cut Menorah from yellow paper and attach to board.
3. Make nine large candles from white paper and nine flames from yellow paper.
4. Attach candles and flames above Menorah.
5. Use a blue marker to write **HANUKKAH** on candles. (Omit center candle.)
6. Attach white letters to board: **FESTIVAL OF LIGHTS**

FLAME PATTERN

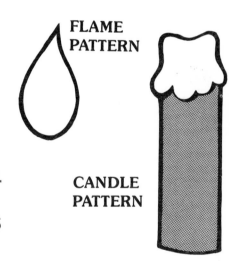

CANDLE PATTERN

An Art Idea!

HAPPY HANUKKAH!

To make:

1. Duplicate a copy of page 51 for each student on white construction paper.
2. Have students:
   a. Color Menorah and candles.
   b. Cut out parts.
   c. Paste candles on Menorah.

Duplicating Page #51

FESTIVAL OF LIGHTS

An Art Idea!

DREIDEL DREIDEL DREIDEL

...A four-sided top!

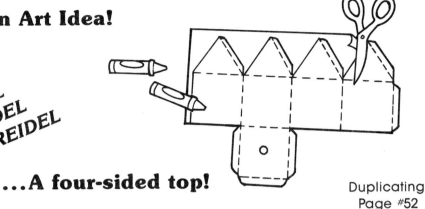

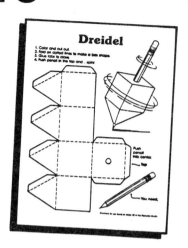

Duplicating
Page #52

To make:
1. Duplicate a copy of page 52 for each student on construction paper.
2. Have students:
   a. Color and cut out.
   b. Fold on dotted lines to make a box.
   c. Glue tabs to close.
   d. Push a pencil in the top and...

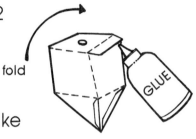

fold

GLUE

SPIN THE DREIDEL!!

A Class Cooking Project!

CHEESE LATKES

Celebrate Hanukkah with a traditional dish...

To make:

CHEESE LATKES

1 cup flour
1/4 cup milk
1/4 teaspoon salt
3 eggs
1 cup cottage cheese
oil for griddle

(makes 20-3" pancakes)

1. Mix all ingredients except oil and flour.
2. Add flour and blend well.
3. Heat oil on griddle.
4. Drop by small amounts on hot griddle.
5. Cook until golden brown; turn like pancakes.

Serve hot with applesauce on top!

DECEMBER

Sunday	Monday	Tuesday	Wednesday	Thursday	Friday	Saturday

Directions for use found on page 4 in the Resource Guide.

STICKERS...

to use with your calendar

Merry Christmas

Spelling Test

Fun Day

Great Day

Happy Hanukkah

Nice Day

Happy Birthday

Test Day

Good Day

Jolly Day

Color, cut and paste on student calendar.

Directions for use found on page 4 in the Resource Guide.

Learning's a Snap!

Name

Date

Bright Things to Glow About!

Name _____ Date _____

You Have a Great Gift!

Chart's Purpose _____ Name _____

Directions for use found on page 5 in the Resource Guide.

DECEMBER'S
Help-at-Home
Activity
Calendar

Below is a learning activity to share with your child each day in December.

1. Have your child name a word that begins with each letter in D E C E M B E R.
2. Go to the library and check out holiday books.
3. Look up five holiday words in the dictionary.
4. Say Christmas words. Have your child say Ho! for the number of syllables. Example: rein-deer = Ho! Ho!
5. Help your child start to memorize part or all of "The Night Before Christmas".
6. Have your child write (or dictate) a letter to Santa.
7. Have your child find Christmas ads in the newspaper.
8. Ask your child to think of holiday compound words. Example: fire/place
9. Have your child think of a Christmas gift that begins with each letter in C H R I S T M A S.
10. Let your child make homemade Christmas cards for family and friends with paper, glitter and glue.
11. Make a holiday gift list with your child.
12. Have your child write a holiday poem.
13. Give your child "Christmas" math problems.
    Example: 3 candy canes + 9 gingerbread men = How many sweets?
14. Read a Christmas story to your child. Ask your child to tell the story in his/her words.
15. Help your child make a Santa puppet with a small paper bag, cotton (beard) and red and black crayons.
16. Have your child color and cut strips of paper. Glue in links for tree chains.
17. Have a family sing-a-long of Christmas songs.
18. Make popcorn together. Help your child string corn for Christmas tree.
19. Go Christmas shopping with your child.
20. Let your child write a Christmas menu.
21. Have your child cut Christmas words from the newspaper.
22. Have your child make a list of or tell things in the house which are red and green.
23. Tell your child about your favorite childhood Christmas.
24. Let your child read or tell a Christmas story to the family at bedtime.
25. Tell Christmas memories around dinner table.
26. Make a tape of family Christmas greetings. Save for your child.
27. Help your child make a list of his/her Christmas gifts. Write thank you notes.
28. Buy your child a calendar for the coming New Year.
29. Help your child set goals for the New Year.
30. Have your child draw his/her favorite part of the year.
31. Have family members make New Year's resolutions.

Directions for use found on page 5 in the Resource Guide.

Dear Santa,

Your friend,

Unscramble and write.

Santa's List

4 2 1 3
n o h r
□ _____

2 3 4 1
o l l d
□ _____

2 4 1 3
r m d u
□ _____

1 5 3 2 4
p y p u p
□ _____

4 2 5 3 1
i r n a t
□ _____

4 1 2 3
e g a m
□ _____

Word Search

Find each word in the puzzle. Use the correct color to circle each word.

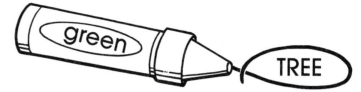

tree-**green**   toy-**purple**
gift-**purple**   holly-**green**
bell-**brown**   sled-**black**
card-**red**   candy-**red**
snow-**blue**   candle-**yellow**

T	R	E	E	C	G
G	I	F	T	A	T
H	V	X	R	N	O
O	C	A	N	D	Y
L	A	B	E	L	L
L	R	S	L	E	D
Y	D	S	N	O	W

Reindeer Antlers

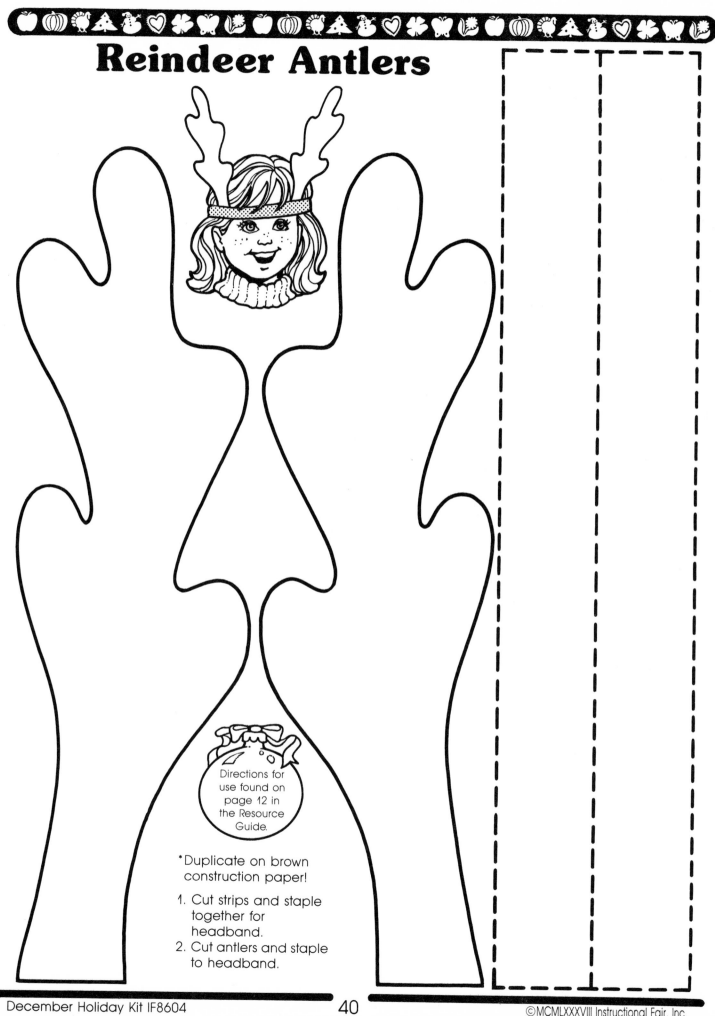

Directions for use found on page 12 in the Resource Guide.

*Duplicate on brown construction paper!

1. Cut strips and staple together for headband.
2. Cut antlers and staple to headband.

Santa's Workshop

Sometimes in the Christmas rush Santa's workshop gets a little mixed up! Help straighten things up again!

☐ Put a red circle around each hidden gift.

☐ Color each hidden elf.

☐ Use green to underline the hidden stockings.

☐ Color each hidden toy.

☐ Put a red check on the hidden parts of Santa's suit.

☐ Count each group of hidden pictures. Write the number in each box.

Directions for use found on page 14 in the Resource Guide.

SANTA PAPER BAG PUPPET

Color the pieces. Cut and paste on small paper bag.

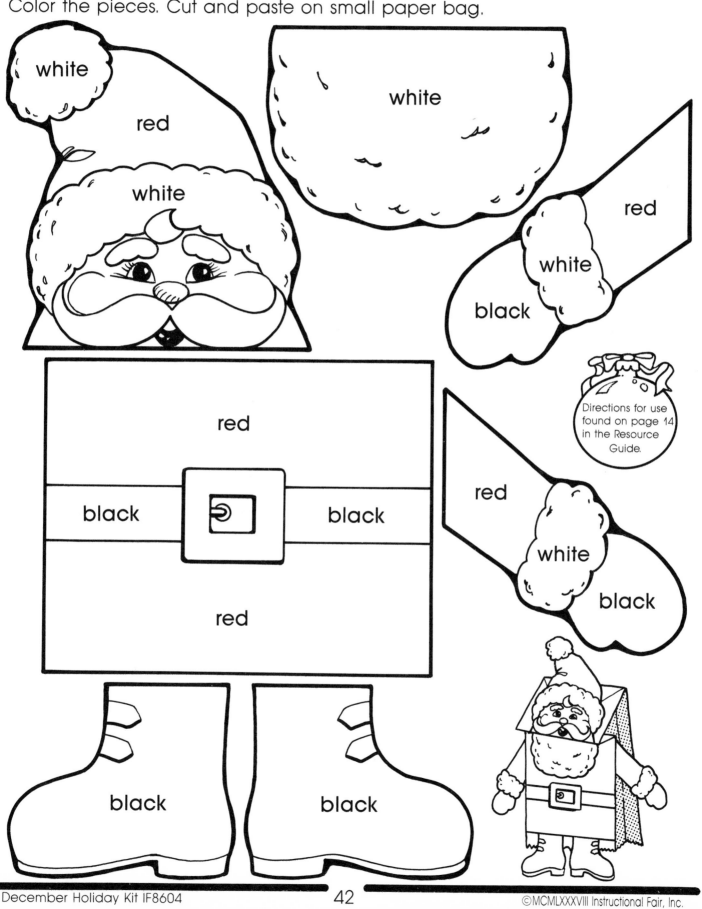

white

red

white

white

red

white

black

red

Directions for use found on page 14 in the Resource Guide.

red

black

black

red

red

white

black

black

black

Stocking Stuffers!

Color and cut out the stocking and stuffers.
Cut the slit in the stocking top.
As you earn each one, glue it in the stocking slit.

Directions for use found on page 16 in the Resource Guide.

Cut.

Name

A LONG WINTER'S NAP

Draw a picture in the bubble of a Christmas Eve dream.
Write a story about the dream on the lines below.

Draw.

A CHRISTMAS EVE DREAM

_____

_____

_____

_____

_____

_____

_____

_____

_____

_____

_____

Directions for use found on page 22 in the Resource Guide.

Crossword Puzzle

Find the word to match each picture. Write the word in the correct squares of the puzzle.

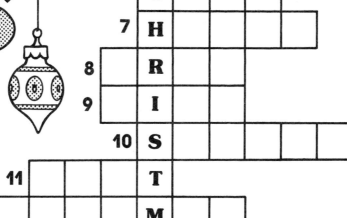

1. M
2. E
3. M E R R Y
4. R
5. Y

6. C
7. H
8. R
9. I
10. S
11. T
12. M
13. A
14. S

☐ **Check each word as you use it.**

☐ bell ☐ sleigh ☐ cane ☐ gift
☐ star ☐ wreath ☐ ring ☐ gingerbread
☐ tree ☐ snowman ☐ toy ☐ holly
☐ mouse ☐ candle

Directions for use found on page 25 in the Resource Guide.

45

Christmas Contractions

Color the holly leaves green. Color the berries red. Cut and paste the berries to show the correct contractions.

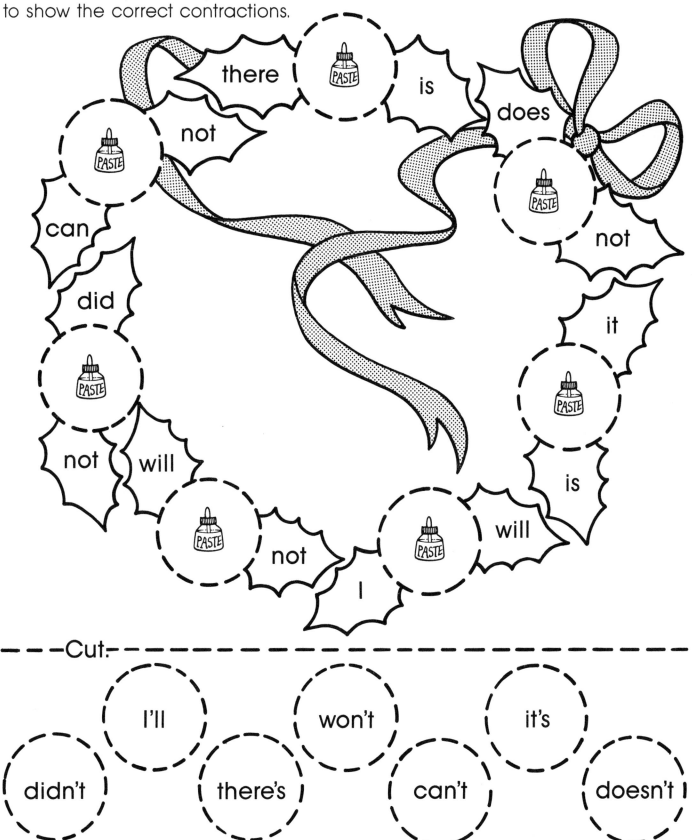

------Cut.------

POP-UP CHRISTMAS CARD

Place inside folded piece of construction paper.

tab →

fold →

tab →

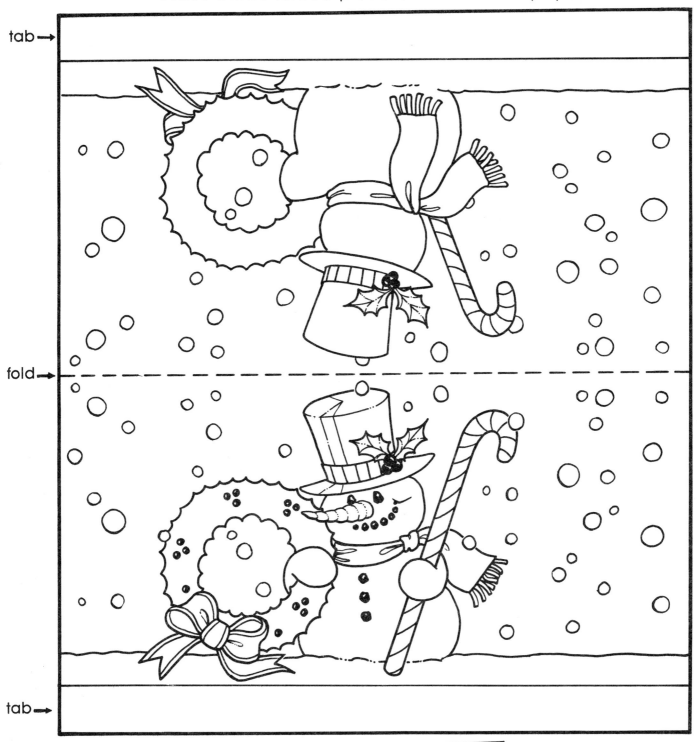

Directions:
1. Color and cut the card.
2. Fold on dotted line.
3. Glue the tabs on each side of the
   inside crease of the construction paper.
4. Fold card closed and decorate card cover.
5. On inside of card write holiday message and sign.

Paste.

Write message.

Directions for use found on page 26 in the Resource Guide.

On the first day of Christmas
My true love gave to me

A partridge in a pear tree.

On the second day of Christmas
My true love gave to me

Two turtle doves.

On the third day of Christmas
My true love gave to me

Three French hens.

On the fourth day of Christmas
My true love gave to me

Four colly birds.

On the fifth day of Christmas
My true love gave to me

Five golden rings.

On the sixth day of Christmas
My true love gave to me

Six geese a-laying.

On the seventh day of Christmas
My true love gave to me

Seven swans a-swimming.

On the tenth day of Christmas
My true love gave to me

Ten lords a-leaping.

On the eighth day of Christmas
My true love gave to me

Eight maids a-milking.

On the eleventh day of Christmas
My true love gave to me

Eleven pipers piping.

On the ninth day of Christmas
My true love gave to me

Nine ladies dancing.

On the twelfth day of Christmas
My true love gave to me

Twelve drummers drumming.

Color border, cut out book frame. Glue on heavy stock or cardboard. Cut book cover at bottom of page. Fold. Place pictures from pages 48 and 49 between covers. Staple. Attach book in center of book frame.

Directions for use found on page 28 in the Resource Guide.

↙ BOOK FRAME

Attach
book
here.

12 DAYS OF

fold

CHRISTMAS

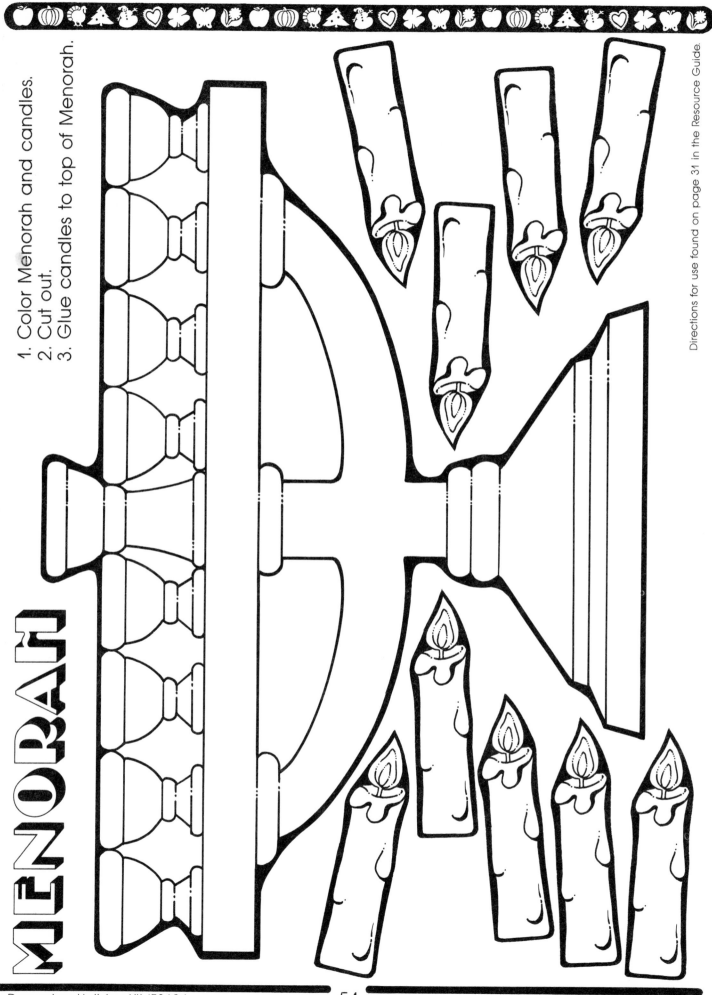

MENORAH

1. Color Menorah and candles.
2. Cut out.
3. Glue candles to top of Menorah.

Directions for use found on page 31 in the Resource Guide.

Dreidel

1. Color and cut out.
2. Fold on dotted lines to make a box shape.
3. Glue tabs to close.
4. Push pencil in the top and…spin!

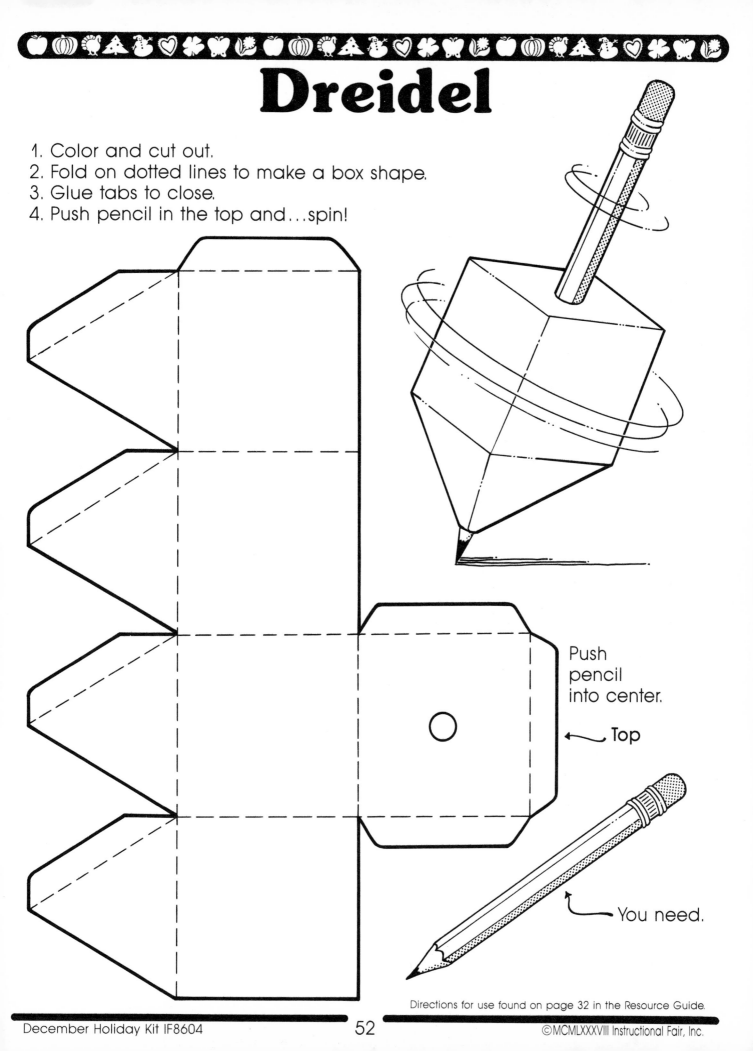

Push pencil into center.

← Top

You need.

Directions for use found on page 32 in the Resource Guide.

A Time for Sharing

A Time for Caring

A Time for Giving

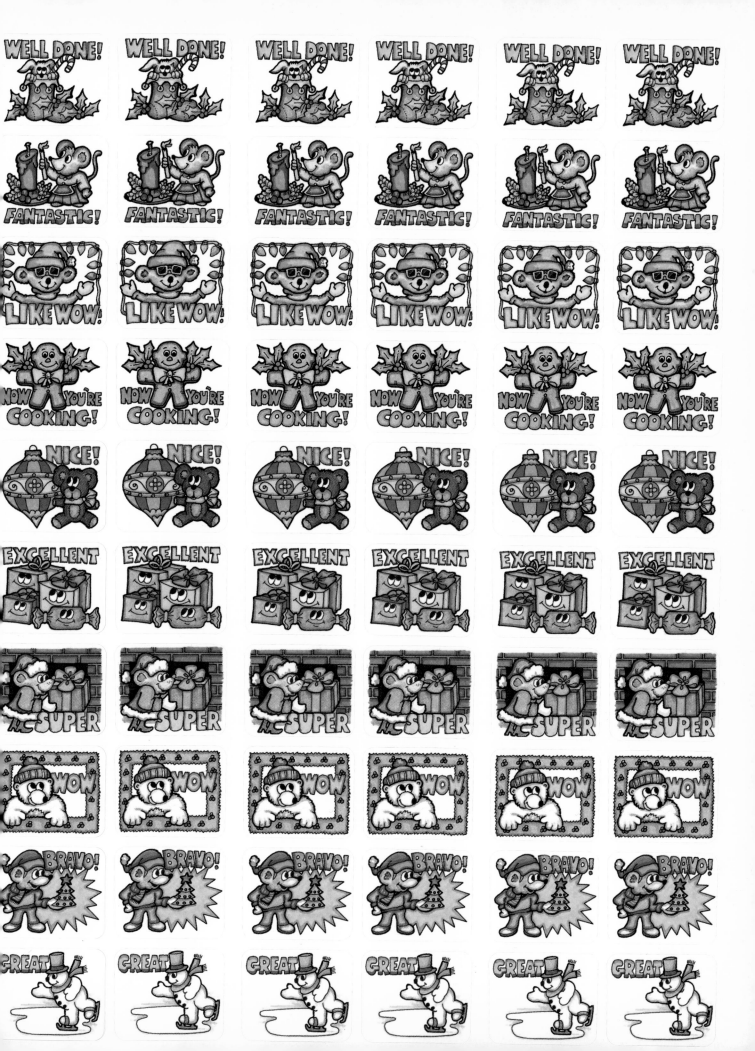